For Sophie, my raison d'etre

2

101 Things to Do When the Kids Finally Leave!

When I started researching this book (and when I say "re-searching", I mean sitting on my couch with a glass of wine and an iPad googling "what to do when the kids leave"), and found all of these entries for something called "empty nest syndrome." There is actually a syndrome. Who knew? Well, this is the U.S., so we have a syndrome for everything. God help us if we aren't diagnosed with something. But I digress…

I've never been one to shy away from change. I guess the flip side of that is I bore easily. When my daughter started kindergarten, there was an actual room set up for mothers overcome by emotion at seeing their little darlings leave for a few hours. A whole room stocked with tissues and tea. Wow. I had the date circled in red on my calendar for months with the words "Independence Day!" written in the box. I celebrated with waffles and silence that morning. And my daughter was appointed line leader so everyone had a good day.

Maybe I'm a bad mom for looking at her independence as a blessing rather than a burden, although I don't think so. My kid doesn't think so. She has turned out relatively normal despite my best efforts. I'm thrilled she is finally leaving to go conquer the world without me hovering in the background, I'm excited about the freedom I'm about to have dropped in my lap, and I'm terrified that now there are no more excuses. No more excuses to do everything I set out to do when I set out to conquer the world.

No more excuses. Live out loud, and do it now.

SH
Orlando, Florida
2014

#1

Drink your coffee.

*Before it gets cold. In the nude. In fact,
new standing rule.., do everything in
the nude.*

#2

Nap.

*I dearly hope no explanation is need-
ed for this one. Nap anytime the
spirit moves you.*

10

#3

Stay out all night.

This, of course, is easier if you have heeded #2, Nap. Go ahead and be reckless, watch the sun rise after a whole night of fun. No one is watching.

#4

Have sex.

In the dining room. Or really any room, other than the bedroom. Bedroom sex is so yesterday.

14

#5

Go ahead and wear the slutty top.

Wear it out. Enjoy the attention.

#6

Don't worry about brushing
your teeth after sneaking a
cigarette on the back porch.

*I know, I know, you haven't smoked since
college. Yeah. Me neither.*

#7

Smoke a joint.

I know, I know, you haven't smoked since college. Yeah. Me neither.

#8

Buy the good cookies.

*And know that you will get to eat
them all. Even the last one.*

#9

Go to the beach for the weekend.

This week-end. Yes. Tomorrow. Go pack your suit and flip-flops. I'll wait.

#10

Delete all reality TV from your DVR.

And fill it with Dowton Abbey. Go ahead... you know you want to.

26

#11

Get a dog.

They're great.

#12

Don't get a cat.

They're not so great. They'll eat your face off.

#13

Leave your husband.

Finally. I know there are husbands out there who are keepers, but on the off chance that yours isn't one of them, consider dumping his ass already. Boyfriends are way more convenient, and you can tell them to leave.

#14

Get a tattoo.

Start small and discreet. Secret acts of rebellion are so damn fun. But for the love of God though, spell check it. Don't have any regerts.

34

#15

Go to Italy.

Skip Rome. go straight to Florence. Walk the same streets that Michelangelo did. Eat gelato every day. Buy shoes and bags. You won't regret it.

#16

Learn to speak Italian.

Perhaps the most glorious language in the world, and particularly impractical. Italy is the only country where it is spoken. But really, if you have a country like Italy, you don't really need another.

#17

Don't do laundry.

For a month. I mean, how dirty do you really get?

40

#18

Date someone inappropriate.

Think stereotypes. Biker, musician, surfer. I'm not saying date him for a long time, just satisfy the fantasy.

#19

Pierce something.

Not something important for goodnes sake! Just an ear or a nostril or maybe a belly button if you don't suffer from mommy belly.

#20

Don't volunteer.

For anything. You've done your time
sister. Enjoy,

#21

Join a book club.

Anything that involves wine, women and potluck is a winner.

#22

Quit your book club.

If they actually expect you to, you know, read stuff.

#23

Start with dessert.

Ummm... yeah. Duh.

#24

Come home from work.

*And don't immediately start cooking
dinner, doing laundry or cleaning
the kitchen.*

#25

Play their Xbox.

All freaking day.

56

#26

Come home.

*And find your house in the exact
same condition it was when you left.*

#27

Sing out loud.

Preferably to Neil Diamond.

#28

Spend the evening by candlelight.

And just stare at yourself in the mirror. You look fabulous!

#29

Buy a round.

For the whole bar. Go at 2 pm on a Tuesday.

#30

Say yes.

Say yes to opportunity. Say yes to joy. Say yes to laughter, to love, to silliness, to challenge, to strength, to friendship, to chances, to second chances, to dessert, to naps, to forgiveness, and kindness.

#31

Start a blog.

I'm sure you have something to say.
go ahead and say it.

#32

Discover a new band.

And become their most loyal groupie.

#33

Eat the last slice of pizza.

You know, the one with the black olives that YOU like.

#34

Redecorate their room.

*To whatever the hell YOU want.
They can sleep on an air mattress if
they come home for a visit, and it
certainly discourages them moving*

#35

Read a book.

In the living room. Naked. For as long as you want.

#36

Sleep late.

Without needing an excuse.

78

#37

Eat what you want for dinner.

Every night. Be your own picky eater.

#38

Have morning sex.

On a Tuesday.

#39

Go to happy hour.

And speak with an accent.

#40

Go blond.

We do have a helluva lot of fun.

#41

Go commando.

Anywhere, Everywhere.

#42

Unplug.

It is freeing.

#43

Buy yourself flowers.

God knows you deserve them.

#44

Be in a parade.

*Doesn't matter which one, although
the gay pride ones are a hoot!*

94

#45

Take a chance.

On yourself. What's the worst that can happen?

#46

Buy the nice sheets.

Egyptian cotton, high thread count,
that match. Indulge.

#47

Start wearing your tiara more.

What? You don't have a tiara? I'll wait while you go buy one...

#48

Give up your Costco membership.

Industrial sized packages of toilet paper, laundry detergent and cereal are a thing of the past.

#49

Learn how to drive a stick shift.

It's time.

#50

Reconsider your choices.

Whichever ones you think need rethinking

#51

Attend ComiCon.

In costume.

#52

Be silly.

Don't worry about what everyone else thinks. No one is as cool as you.

#53

Run a 5k.

Or not.

#54

Learn to salsa dance.

Just. Do. It. You won't regret it.

#55

Do a shot.

It doesn't need to be tequila. Try a yummy one. Salted chocolate pretzel, lemon drop, red-headed slut...

#56

Pick up a man.

Don't take him home or anything (heavens no!). Just pick him up, and then excuse yourself to go to the ladies room and sneak out.

#57

Skip church.

If you're doing this right there will already be a few things you feel guilty about on Sunday morning.

#58

Ride a Harley.

Trust me on this. Just do it.

122

#59

Take a yoga class.

Or not.

124

#60

Watch the sun rise.

After a great night, don't wake up early for that shit.

126

#61

Forgive someone.

Or not.

#62

Google your high school ex.

And laugh and laugh.

#63

Call in sick.

*When you aren't sick. Especially
when you aren't.*

132

#64

Listen to the silence.

Shhhhh.....

#65

Leave your vibrator on top of the night-stand.

Every damn day.

#66

Have loud sex.

Whenever the hell you want.

#67

Skinny dip.

In fact, don't even bother with bath-ing suits ever again. I mean, what's the point?

#68

Paint your kitchen.

Tomato red. Blueberry blue. Broccoli green. Just. Not. Beige. Your beige days are over baby.

#69

Start scrapbooking.

It can be a wonderful way to record your memories.... oh shit I can't do this... laughing too hard... still laughing... scrapbooking! Ha!

#70

Buy a sports car.

And don't let them drive it when they come home on break.

#71

Say no.

*To whatever, whenever you want.
Practice in the mirror so you feel
comfortable. No you can't volun-
teer at the luncheon, no you can't
chair the fundraising committee,
no you can't give up your week-
end to babysit, no you can't let
them borrow your car, no, no, no.
Learn to say no to the things that
don't matter so you can say yes to
the things that do.*

#72

Finally lose the last of the baby weight.

You deserve to look and feel as fabulous as you are.

#73

Date a younger man.

Or not. They have their positive qualities as long as they don't talk too much. Shhh baby... just keep nibbling....

152

#74

Sleep with both eyes closed.

At the same time.

#75

Stop caring whether they are wearing a hat in cold weather.

Not your job anymore.

#76

Spend Sunday in your jammies.

Or nothing at all. Your call.

#77

Go paintballing.

Shooting shit is fun! Feel free to make little "pew pew" sounds as you do it.

#78

Admire the new baby.

Then leave. Because you can. And laugh and laugh

#79

Get in your car and just drive.

Without first having to turn the radio down, change the station, move the seat back, throw out all the soda cups, and wonder what the hell splilled.

#80

Set up an internet dating profile.

And then just mess with them.

#81

Never, ever, ever go to a school concert, program, or open house again.

Can I have an amen?

#82

Go back to school.

This sounds like a serious thing, and it kinda is. It doesn't need to be something job related, it can be art history, web design, creative writing... whatever flips your skirt. Allow your mind to wander to interesting places.

#83

Sleep in the nude.

If you aren't already. No more worries about someone waking you in the middle of the night because their throat is sore or they heard a noise.

#83

Swear like a sailor.

Get creative. Fuckity, fuck, fuck.

#84

Live your life.

Without ever having to see another fucking eye roll. I hate those. I SO hate those. Don't you?

#85

Be your own tech support.

You're on your own now... learn how to use your phone, your laptop, your tablet and the remote. It will only hurt for a little while.

#86

No more mood roulette.

You can come home not wondering what kind of beast you will find on your couch.

#87

Never get angry again about the socks left on the floor or the dishes left in the sink.

Cause their yours.

#88

Flash someone.

Go ahead, make their day.

#89

Only take care of your calendar.

They're big boys and girls now, they can remember when they need to get their hair cut.

#90

Wake up in the morning.

And not worry about waking anyone else up.

#91

Start checking things off your bucket list.

Now is the time... a bucket list is more than a movie, its a way of life.

#92

Downsize.

There are so many better things to do than clean a big house, and there are so many better things to spend your money on than maintaining a big house. Set yourself up in a condo or a cottage and use your time and money the way YOU want to.

#93

Rediscover a passion.

For me it has been designing and sewing... for you it might be traveling, painting, photography, cooking, writing... with the experience of more living behind you, your work might have more depth, meaning and power.

#94

Reinvent your look.

It happens, we become moms. We stop dressing up and start dressing for comfort, we allow our hair to be "wash and go", our idea of make up is lip gloss and mascara, and yet when we look in the mirror, we know that isn't really us. Remember who you used to be... sassy, sexy, fierce. Yes, you can be all of those things, no matter what your age. Don't give up on yourself,

#95

Be selfish.

Not all the time, and not with every-thing, just some things. Never feel guilty for keeping some things and some time just for you.

#96

Don't compromise anymore

You've put your needs and dreams on hold for a many years to raise them, now it is time to put yours first. They will adapt, don't worry.

#97

Follow your kid on social media.

It's the only way you're going to know what is going on in their lives. Feel free to embarrass them every once in a while... there are some parenting roles that we never

#98

Realize that all choices are still open...

A good friend of mine, age 47. dreamed of changing careers. He had remarried and told his new wife of his dream... but then said "but I woud be 51 when I graduated with the degree." And she responded "and how old will you be in four years if you don't get the degree?" Don't use your age as an excuse not to follow your dreams.

#99

Give up control.

And see where it takes you.

#100

Pee with the door open.

Don't think an explanation is warranted with this one.

#101

Allow yourself some tears.

But not too many, there are mountains to climb, songs to sing, shoes to wear, dances to dance, adventures to plan, cakes to bake, love to make, jokes to tell, books to read, fears to conquer, beauty queens to mock, ice cream to be tasted, styles to rock, boys to kiss, and a life to live. Out loud.

7483122R00117

Printed in Great Britain
by Amazon.co.uk, Ltd.,
Marston Gate.